ROBIN 1

It is a long time ago in England. There are kings and princes, good people and bad people, rich people and poor people.

Richard the First, King of England, is a brave and good man, but his brother, Prince John, is not. Prince John is rich but many of his people are not. 'The people must pay more taxes,' he says to the Sheriff of Nottingham. 'Some of them can't pay,' says the Sheriff. 'Then take their houses and animals away from them!' says Prince John.

Robin of Locksley is another brave and good man. He hears about Prince John and the Sheriff of Nottingham and he is angry. 'I must do something to help the people without homes or money,' he says.

But this is not easy, and soon Robin is in danger – very great danger.

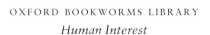

OXFORD BOOKWORMS LIBRARY

Human Interest

Robin Hood

Starter (250 headwords)

JOHN ESCOTT

Robin Hood

Illustrated by
Bob Harvey
Pennant Inc

OXFORD UNIVERSITY PRESS

OXFORD
UNIVERSITY PRESS

Great Clarendon Street, Oxford OX2 6DP

Oxford University Press is a department of the University of Oxford.
It furthers the University's objective of excellence in research, scholarship,
and education by publishing worldwide in

Oxford New York

Auckland Cape Town Dar es Salaam Hong Kong Karachi
Kuala Lumpur Madrid Melbourne Mexico City Nairobi
New Delhi Shanghai Taipei Toronto

With offices in

Argentina Austria Brazil Chile Czech Republic France Greece
Guatemala Hungary Italy Japan Poland Portugal Singapore
South Korea Switzerland Thailand Turkey Ukraine Vietnam

OXFORD and OXFORD ENGLISH are registered trade marks of
Oxford University Press in the UK and in certain other countries

ISBN: 978 0 19 423416 0

Printed in Hong Kong

Word count (main text): 960

For more information on the Oxford Bookworms Library, visit
www.oup.com/bookworms

CONTENTS

STORY INTRODUCTION   i

Robin Hood   1

GLOSSARY   25

ACTIVITIES: Before Reading   29

ACTIVITIES: While Reading   30

ACTIVITIES: After Reading   32

ABOUT THE AUTHOR   34

ABOUT THE BOOKWORMS LIBRARY   35

Richard the First is King of England. He is a brave, good man, and the people love him. They call him Richard the Lionheart.

But when the King goes away, his brother Prince John does his work...

Sheriff of Nottingham, the people must pay more taxes!

Then take their houses and animals away from them!

But Prince John, some of them can't pay.

One day, a young boy is hunting in the forest. He kills a deer. But some of the Sheriff's men are watching him...

A day or two later...

There's a shooting contest in Nottingham. The winner gets a silver arrow!

That's very interesting.

I'm afraid, Robin. Why does the Sheriff want to have a contest? Perhaps he wants to catch you.

I know. But I must win the contest for the people of Nottingham.

On the day of the contest...

Forty men shoot their arrows.

Three men hit their targets in the centre – Sir Guy Gisborne, one of the Sheriff's men, and an old man with a beard. They shoot again.

This time, the Sheriff's man and Sir Guy do badly.

But the old man's arrow hits the centre!

I don't have my silver arrow. I must go back and get it one day. Ha! Ha! Ha!

Sir Guy Gisborne visits Lord Fitzwalter.

Listen, Fitzwalter. I want to marry your daughter, Lady Marian.

Oh!

No! I can never marry him! He's a bad man, and I love Robin.

I must go away.

I understand, my daughter. But Sir Guy can make things bad for us.

Yes, my daughter.

Lady Marian tells Robin about Sir Guy ...

...and I can never marry him! Not in a hundred years! I love you, Robin.

And I love you, Marian. You must stay in Sherwood Forest with me.

A week later, Robin and Marian get married in Sherwood Forest.

We must fight for everything that is good and right. When King Richard come back to England, he must know that we are his true friends.

GLOSSARY

brave   not afraid

carry   take someone or something from one place to another

catch   get and keep someone or something

contest   something which somebody tries to win

fight   go against somebody and stop him or her doing something

friar   someone who works for the Catholic church

hang   kill somebody by holding him above the ground with a rope round his neck

hide   go to a place where people cannot find you

idea   a new thought or plan

king   a man who is head of a country

marry   make someone your wife or husband

outlaw   someone who breaks the law and hides

pay   give money to someone for something

prince   the son of a king or queen

rich (*adj*)   someone with a lot of money is rich

sheriff   somebody who stops people breaking the law

silver   an expensive metal

summer   a warm time of the year

taxes   money that the government takes from you

thief   someone who takes something that is not theirs

traitor   someone who goes against his king or his country

wake   stop sleeping

win   do better than any of the others in a contest

Robin Hood

ACTIVITIES

ACTIVITIES

Before Reading

1 Look at the front cover and choose the correct answer for these questions.

1 When do you think this story happens?
   a ☐ Today.
   b ☐ In the past.
   c ☐ In a time that is to come.

2 Where do you think this story happens?
   a ☐ In America.
   b ☐ In England.
   c ☐ In Japan.
   d ☐ In Australia.

2 Read the back cover of the book and answer these questions.

1 Do you think Prince John is a good man or bad man?
2 Do you think Robin Hood is a good man or bad man?
3 What happens to Robin Hood, do you think?

ACTIVITIES

While Reading

1 Read pages 1–3, then answer these questions.

1 What do the people call Richard, the King of England?
2 Where is Robin's house?
3 The Sheriff of Nottingham tells his soldiers to bring Robin to the castle. How does Robin hear about this?
4 Why can't Robin marry Lady Marian?

2 Read pages 4–9. Who says or thinks these words?

1 'We must take money from Prince John's bad men.'
2 'Wait for me to come across!'
3 'This is Robin Hood!'
4 'Wake up! I want you to carry me across the river.'
5 'Now you can carry me – across the river again!'

3 Read pages 10–15, and then answer these questions.

1 Who is 'a good friend of Lady Marian Fitzwalter'?
2 Why is this friend hiding from the Sheriff?
3 Why is the boy hunting in the forest?
4 What do the soldiers say is to happen to the boy the next day?
5 Who is the 'woman' carrying eggs?
6 Who tells the boy to run to the forest?

4 **Read pages 16–18. Are these sentences true (T) or false (F)?**

1 The winner of the shooting contest gets a gold arrow.
2 The Sheriff wants to catch Friar Tuck.
3 Robin wants to win the contest for the people
  of Nottingham.
4 Forty men shoot in the contest.
5 Sir Guy Gisborne wins the contest.

5 **Before you read pages 20–24, can you guess what happens to these characters?**

Robin

☐ He kills Sir Guy Gisborne.
☐ He marries Lady Marian.
☐ He leaves the forest and goes back to his home.

Sir Guy Gisborne

☐ He marries Lady Marian.
☐ He catches all of Robin's men.
☐ He leaves England.

Prince John

☐ He marries Lady Marian.
☐ He kills Robin.
☐ He becomes king.

Lady Marian

☐ She comes to live in the forest with Robin.
☐ She marries Prince John to help Robin.
☐ She leaves England.

ACTIVITIES

After Reading

1 Use these words to join the sentences together.

but   gets   from   in   and

1 King Richard is a good man. The people love him.
2 The soldiers come after Robin. He hides from them in the forest.
3 The Sheriff and Sir Guy look down. A castle window.
4 The shooting contest winner. A silver arrow.
5 The men hit their targets. The centre.

2 Complete this summary of the story. Use these words:

taxes   kill   outlaw   marry   forest
brother   friends   money   hide   hungry

King Richard the First goes away. His .... is Prince John. Prince John wants the people to pay more .... Robin of Locksley is going to .... Lady Marian, but somebody tells him, 'They want to .... you. You must ....!' So Robin goes to Sherwood Forest. Now he is an .... There are more men hiding in the forest. They and Robin take .... from Prince John's bad men. They wait in the ...., then stop rich people and say, 'We want money for the .... people.' They want King Richard to know that they are his true ....

3 Look at each picture, then answer the questions after it.

1 Who is getting into the boat?

2 Who is this?

3 Who is this and
  what is happening?

4 Who is sitting in the water?

5 Who is this?

6 Who are these two people?

ABOUT THE AUTHOR

John Escott worked in business before becoming a writer. He has written many books for readers of all ages, but enjoys writing crime and mystery thrillers most of all. He was born in Somerset, in the west of England, but now lives in Bournemouth, on the south coast. When he is not working, he likes looking for old books in small back-street bookshops, watching Hollywood films, and walking for miles along empty beaches.

He has written or retold more than twenty stories for the Oxford Bookworms Library. His original stories include *Star Reporter* (Starter, Human Interest), *Goodbye, Mr Hollywood* (Stage 1, Thriller & Adventure), and *Sister Love and Other Crime Stories* (Stage 1, Crime & Mystery).

OXFORD BOOKWORMS LIBRARY

Classics • Crime & Mystery • Factfiles • Fantasy & Horror
Human Interest • Playscripts • Thriller & Adventure
True Stories • World Stories

The OXFORD BOOKWORMS LIBRARY provides enjoyable reading in English, with a wide range of classic and modern fiction, non-fiction, and plays. It includes original and adapted texts in seven carefully graded language stages, which take learners from beginner to advanced level. An overview is given on the next pages.

All Stage 1 titles are available as audio recordings, as well as over eighty other titles from Starter to Stage 6. All Starters and many titles at Stages 1 to 4 are specially recommended for younger learners. Every Bookworm is illustrated, and Starters and Factfiles have full-colour illustrations.

The OXFORD BOOKWORMS LIBRARY also offers extensive support. Each book contains an introduction to the story, notes about the author, a glossary, and activities. Additional resources include tests and worksheets, and answers for these and for the activities in the books. There is advice on running a class library, using audio recordings, and the many ways of using Oxford Bookworms in reading programmes. Resource materials are available on the website <www.oup.com/bookworms>.

The *Oxford Bookworms Collection* is a series for advanced learners. It consists of volumes of short stories by well-known authors, both classic and modern. Texts are not abridged or adapted in any way, but carefully selected to be accessible to the advanced student.

You can find details and a full list of titles in the *Oxford Bookworms Library Catalogue* and *Oxford English Language Teaching Catalogues*, and on the website <www.oup.com/bookworms>.

THE OXFORD BOOKWORMS LIBRARY
GRADING AND SAMPLE EXTRACTS

STARTER • 250 HEADWORDS

present simple – present continuous – imperative –
can/cannot, must – *going to* (future) – simple gerunds …

Her phone is ringing – but where is it?

Sally gets out of bed and looks in her bag. No phone. She looks under the bed. No phone. Then she looks behind the door. There is her phone. Sally picks up her phone and answers it. ***Sally's Phone***

STAGE 1 • 400 HEADWORDS

… past simple – coordination with *and, but, or* –
subordination with *before, after, when, because, so* …

I knew him in Persia. He was a famous builder and I worked with him there. For a time I was his friend, but not for long. When he came to Paris, I came after him – I wanted to watch him. He was a very clever, very dangerous man. ***The Phantom of the Opera***

STAGE 2 • 700 HEADWORDS

… present perfect – *will* (future) – *(don't) have to, must not, could* –
comparison of adjectives – simple *if* clauses – past continuous –
tag questions – *ask/tell* + infinitive …

While I was writing these words in my diary, I decided what to do. I must try to escape. I shall try to get down the wall outside. The window is high above the ground, but I have to try. I shall take some of the gold with me – if I escape, perhaps it will be helpful later. ***Dracula***

STAGE 3 • 1000 HEADWORDS

... should, may – present perfect continuous – *used to* – past perfect –
causative – relative clauses – indirect statements ...

Of course, it was most important that no one should see
Colin, Mary, or Dickon entering the secret garden. So Colin
gave orders to the gardeners that they must all keep away
from that part of the garden in future. *The Secret Garden*

STAGE 4 • 1400 HEADWORDS

... past perfect continuous – passive (simple forms) –
would conditional clauses – indirect questions –
relatives with *where/when* – gerunds after prepositions/phrases ...

I was glad. Now Hyde could not show his face to the world
again. If he did, every honest man in London would be
proud to report him to the police. *Dr Jekyll and Mr Hyde*

STAGE 5 • 1800 HEADWORDS

... future continuous – future perfect –
passive (modals, continuous forms) –
would have conditional clauses – modals + perfect infinitive ...

If he had spoken Estella's name, I would have hit him. I was so
angry with him, and so depressed about my future, that I could
not eat the breakfast. Instead I went straight to the old house.
Great Expectations

STAGE 6 • 2500 HEADWORDS

... passive (infinitives, gerunds) – advanced modal meanings –
clauses of concession, condition

When I stepped up to the piano, I was confident. It was as if I
knew that the prodigy side of me really did exist. And when I
started to play, I was so caught up in how lovely I looked that
I didn't worry how I would sound. *The Joy Luck Club*

BOOKWORMS · HUMAN INTEREST · STARTER

King Arthur

JANET HARDY-GOULD

It is the year 650 in England. There is war everywhere because the old king is dead and he has no son. Only when the new king comes can the fighting stop and the strange, magical story of King Arthur begin. But first, Merlin the ancient magician has to find a way of finding the next king . . .

BOOKWORMS · HUMAN INTEREST · STARTER

Sally's Phone

CHRISTINE LINDOP

Sally is always running – and she has her phone with her all the time: at home, on the train, at work, at lunchtime, and at the shops.

But then one afternoon suddenly she has a different phone . . . and it changes her life.

BOOKWORMS · HUMAN INTEREST · STARTER

Star Reporter

JOHN ESCOTT

'There's a new girl in town,' says Joe, and soon Steve is out looking for her. Marietta is easy to find in a small town, but every time he sees her something goes wrong . . . and his day goes from bad to worse.

BOOKWORMS · CRIME & MYSTERY · STARTER

Girl on a Motorcycle

JOHN ESCOTT

'Give me the money,' says the robber to the Los Angeles security guard. The guard looks at the gun and hands over the money. The robber has long blond hair and rides a motorcycle – and a girl with long blond hair arrives at Kenny's motel – on a motorcycle. Is she the robber?

BOOKWORMS · HUMAN INTEREST · STAGE 1

A Little Princess

FRANCES HODGSON BURNETT

Retold by Jennifer Bassett

Sara Crewe is a very rich little girl. She first comes to England when she is seven, and her father takes her to Miss Minchin's school in London. Then he goes back to his work in India. Sara is very sad at first, but she soon makes friends at school.

But on her eleventh birthday, something terrible happens, and now Sara has no family, no home, and not a penny in the world . . .

BOOKWORMS · CRIME & MYSTERY · STAGE 1

Sister Love and Other Crime Stories

JOHN ESCOTT

Some sisters are good friends, some are not. Sometimes there is more hate in a family than there is love. Karin is beautiful and has lots of men friends, but she can be very unkind to her sister Marcia. Perhaps when they were small, there was love between them, but that was a long time ago.

They say that everybody has one crime in them. Perhaps they only take an umbrella that does not belong to them. Perhaps they steal from a shop, perhaps they get angry and hit someone, perhaps they kill . . .